Sit in it

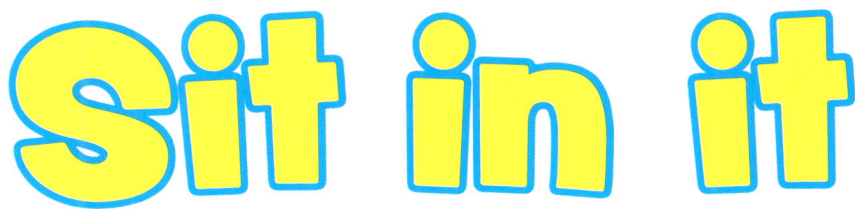

Written by Catherine Baker

Collins

tip in it

tap it in

sit in it

tip in

sit

sip it

tip

12

tap tip sip

15

Review: After reading

Use your assessment from hearing the children read to choose any GPCs or words that need additional practice.

Read 1: Decoding
- Ask the children to read the following. Check that they sound talk and blend as they read the words aloud.

    sit   in   it   tap

- Ask the children to read page 8. Ask: Can you blend in your head silently before you read these words aloud?

Read 2: Prosody
- Model reading pages 8 and 9 using a natural, speech-like tone. Show the children how you can use your voice to make the words **tip in** sound exciting.
- Ask the children to copy your reading.
- Challenge them to read page 4 in a similar way, making it sound exciting.

Read 3: Comprehension
- Ask the children which activity in the book they would like to do most, and why. Ask: Have you ever been to a fair or amusement park? What did you enjoy doing there?
- Use the pictures on pages 14 and 15 to model how to recap the content of the book. Work together to make an exciting oral caption for each image. (e.g. *Splash down at the water slide!*) Do not write any captions.
- Bonus content:
    - Look at the pictures on the poster on pages 2 and 3. Discuss together what is happening in each picture.
    - Turn to pages 12 and 13. Read the title. Ask: Which of the rides looks most exciting? Which tips up the most?